About the Author

For many years I wanted to open a children's clothing boutique. Between marriage, children and divorce, it seems like the time was never right. But… "when is the RIGHT time?" I woke up one morning and said to myself "I must take this single parent thing head on and make it work". I decided that I was not going to disappoint my children and would make being a single parent my priority.

In 1999 when my youngest was 2 years old, I decided to buy a journal and I wrote in that journal almost every day. I wrote my future goals and I also wrote prayers to God. I knew one day God would make all of it possible for me to achieve.

I drew how I wanted my boutique to look. As my children got older and life kept happening for us, I would have a monthly goal of just planning. What I kept in my mind was that my children would not be babies forever! I would even add up the years of how old I would be when the last child left home. As years went by I would try to come up with ideas of how I would make this all happen. I called that the planning process.

During my planning it seemed very easy as I wrote every detail that came through to my mind. I wrote every detail as it came to me.
The reason I decided to write this book was to help others who are trying to open a mobile boutique. On my journey, I did my research on how to open a brick and mortar. The overhead cost of a brick and mortar was out of the range I was willing to pay. Also, on my journey, there were times I got discouraged, but with prayer and the support of my best friend I kept my head above water. My hope is that this informational book will give you guidance on how to start your own mobile boutique.
Happy reading and God Bless!

Norma Sabrina Linen

Disclaimer

The information contained in this book is for informational purposes only.

It is important that you understand that I am not a lawyer or an accountant. Any legal or financial advice that I give is my opinion based on my own experiences. Any amount of earnings disclosed in this guide should not be considered average.

Any similarities with people or facts are unintentional.

While every attempt has been made to verify the information provided here, the author and the publisher cannot assume any responsibility for errors, inaccuracies or omissions.

While the author and publisher of this course have made their best effort to ensure it is useful, informative and valuable, the author and publisher make no representation or warranties with regard to the accuracy, applicability, or completeness of the contents of this course; furthermore, they do not accept any liability for any direct or indirect losses or damages arising directly or indirectly through the use of any material or information contained within this course.
Your level of success in attaining the results claimed in this course and related materials depends on the time you devote to the ideas and techniques mentioned. Since these factors differ according to individuals, we cannot guarantee your success or income level, nor are we responsible for any of your actions.

It is my desire and obligation to inform you that there are affiliate links contained in this guide that I may benefit from financially.

I do not assume responsibility or liability for any third party material or opinions contained in this book. The publication of such third party materials does not constitute my guarantee of any information, instruction, opinion, products or services contained within the third party material. The use of recommended third party material does not guarantee any success and or earnings related to you or your business. Publication of such third party material is simply a recommendation and an expression of my own opinion of that material.

No part of this publication shall be reproduced, transmitted or sold in whole or in part in any form, without the prior written consent of the author. All trademarks and registered trademarks appearing in this book are the property of their respective owners.
Users of this guide are advised to do their own due diligence when it comes to making business decisions and all information, products and services that have been provided should be independently verified by your own qualified professionals. By reading this book, you agree that myself and my company is not responsible for the success or failure of your business decisions relating to any information contained in this guide.

Introduction:

I came from a family of fashion, and it has always played a big part in my family. From the age of about 14 my dreams were to open a children's boutique. I had it all planned, from the size of the boutique, to the color of the fitting room. But… life happened, and my dreams got put on the back burner for many, many years. I'm sure some of my readers can relate to that! It seems like the time was never right according to my plans. At one point it seemed like time would never be right.

Well what I didn't know was that the perfect time was always there, it just wasn't my perfect timing but God's perfect timing. Even though it took me years to put my plans together it never left my heart. I would have dreams about turning the keys to my own children's boutique, I had dreams about being self-employed and having my children work in the boutique. What I didn't know is when I finally launched my business, my children would be adults.

I was inspired to write this book by many of my Boutique customers after they read my testimony on my blog page of my online store. I was inspired by one of my childhood friends Jeannine Britton to share with other mothers who have dreams of opening a business and how it could happen no matter what or how old you may be. In fact, I had to inspire myself as well.

I was the type of person who would almost always say something is too good to be true. Well years of thinking that and believing that it started coming to past. When I realized that I was the main person stopping me is when I started studying the power of words! I stopped believing that things were too good to happen to me and then good things started happening to me.

In the first few chapters I will share my story and then break down the process of opening a mobile boutique without robbing your piggy bank. In this book you will find many helpful and inexpensive materials on how to open a mobile boutique.

I live by Mark 11:23 *For verily I say unto you, That whosoever shall say unto this mountain, Be thou removed, and be thou cast into the sea; and shall not doubt in his heart, but shall believe that those things which he saith shall come to pass; he shall have whatsoever he saith.*

The Beginning

In January 2014, I was on my way to Durham, North Carolina to take my daughter back to college after the Christmas break. On our way I passed a huge flea market, I thought to myself, maybe I could start a consignment store for children instead of having a boutique. I'm a thrift shopper, so many times when I'm at Goodwill there are customers there dropping off thousands of pieces of children items.

I thought why not call up all of my family and friends , and ask them if they have any children clothes they would like to donate? I asked one of my co-workers to donate, she was glad to get rid of her children old clothes. She had friends that heard about me accepting donations, they also wanted to donate.

To help I would go and pick up the items. Some even gave me adult clothes, shoes, toys, books and even tried to give me furniture. I couldn't except furniture because I didn't have space for them. For about 8 month I collected a store full of items, a few times, I went to the flea market but didn't sell like I expected. That didn't stop me. I kept thinking about all these multimillion dollar business owners, who I constantly listens to their stories on podcast. After a while I wasn't feeling the flea market or the used items, but I wasn't giving up.

Opening a consignment shop sound easy at the planning sessions, but once I really got into it, it took a lot of work. The kind of consignment shop I had in mind, was more of a buy and wear idea. Which meant every single piece of clothing would be washed before sold.

For the most part most of the donations were clean, but I washed every piece of clothing just because it was the right thing to do. That got old quick, I was working harder doing laundry than selling them. I even thought about hiring someone to wash and fold them all, but once I looked at my cost, it would cost far more than I was willing to spend.

I said to myself something must change. I did notice when I sold at the flea market most items people had were new to slightly used. I had a small 3-bedroom apartment on the Eastside of Charlotte, NC where I would store all of my donations in one of the spare bedroom. I was getting overwhelmed. Day in and day out I would get calls from people to come pick up donations! It was amazing how quick the word got out that I was looking for used and gently used children clothing, I figured if this is growing so rapidly what other business I could start and have many supporters.

It's Always Ok to Have a Change of Heart

In December of the same year (2014) a coworker told me about a flea market between Charlotte and Monroe, NC. I decided to go that weekend to see what it was all about. I googled the address and it took me to the flea market.I sat in my car debating rather I wanted to stay there or not, right next to the flea market was a cargo trailer dealer shop. When I saw the cargo trailers, I thought about making one of those into a mobile store on wheels selling used children clothes.

I went in and moments later I had the keys to a 2014 Cargo trailer.Talk about someone so excited! Then it came to me that I didn't have a place to park my purchase, nor did I have a truck to pull it. Maybe I should have thought this through before making the purchase! Not really...God had it all planned! it was his timing not mine!
Talking about bad timing,kept coming to my mind. Then

God spoke to me and said, "call your brother, he has all of the equipment you will need to transport your trailer" . I called my brother, who lives 3 hours away. I explained to him what I've done, he laughed and said " Only you". I asked him if he could take some time later in the week to assist me with transporting? He said that his schedule was really busy that week. I got a little discouraged, then I remembered that my daughter who was in college had a Ford Explorer.

I called my Dad to ask what he thought about my daughter's Ford Explorer ? He said that it would pull the trailer, but I would have to purchase a tow package. I spoke to the owner about storage and installing the tow package, he said storage wasn't a problem and they would be able to install the tow package as well.

The day came, and it was time to pick up my trailer. I had to pay for a lighting system for my daughter's SUV, this was also an unexpected bill. Plus the tow package. The dealer installed them both and we were on our way.

My plan was to store it for a few months at my parents' house in South Carolina, but a few months turned into almost 1 year.
I met with my best friend, who is also an awesome business partner. We met so we could discuss how I wanted to design my Boutique. During this time, I still didn't have my boutique in my possession, but the planning was still going forth.

I had to get busy finding a location that would
accommodate my boutique, as well as a planning location. The best thing for me was to look for a place where I would have a large enough space to park my trailer. I took this time to focus on the boutique and what I was going to sell.

One night at our business planning, I decided to google fashion trucks, and it blew my mind to see how many people were doing it. I got really, really, excited and it motivated me. Plus I was living out my passion. So here I am ready to bring you some awesome information. In the next few chapters of my book you will see how to open and operate a mobile boutique. I hope that this book will motivate and inspire you to live out your dreams.

Chapter 1: Your Goals

How to write Goals and what should be included in your Goals!
1. Develop an increased understanding of a Mobile

Fashion Boutique
Learning about the mobile boutique industry is the first step in establishing your goals. I say this because… you need to know what is indeed possible with your mobile boutique in terms of reach and profitability.

If you say your goal is to earn $500,000 next year doing home parties. You should estimate how many shows and how much you will profit, physically possible in a year. You could be setting yourself up for disappointment. No it's not that you can't earn $500,000 in a year running a mobile boutique, but you need to know what's physically possible. You can only do one event at a time on your own. However; this doesn't mean that you can't build your brand and then franchise yourself. This is also not taking internet sales into account which you can do in your sleep!

2. Your goals should be broad but workable. It's one thing to set your goals high, as all the life coaches and gurus say you should set your goals high. It's quite another thing to set goals you can achieve. I advise that your start with your first goals being centered around making your first sale. From there you can set goals according to the confidence you got from realizing you could actually sell something to someone.

3. Your goals should have intentions (aim or plan) You shouldn't set your goals because everyone sets goals. Your goal setting campaign should be based on pushing your overall vision forward. This means you need an overall vision that can be broken down into attainable goals.

4. Your goals should be intangible (unable to be touched or grasped) What I mean by this is that you need to set goals that are currently out of reach. Goals that will take considerable effort to achieve. If it's not a next-level goal, don't set it. Your goals should be abstract(existing in thought or as an idea but not having a physical or concrete existence).

Once you've reached one of your goals, celebrate and then move on to the next one. You will find that your entrepreneurial journey is more about the journey than it is the destination.

When writing your goals there are certain keywords you will be dealing with, such as planning a goal everyday and stick with it no matter what. This will not only make you a great planner, but will also show consistency.When most people hear the word goals they think it's just as simple as writing a plan for a blocked time and try to master it. Well it's not that simple.Goals are you planning for your future and your business!

Sometimes you will find yourself feeling overwhelmed and tired, but having goals to go by will give you that guidance and focused mind to keep pushing. We all know that life happens, it can take us off of our focus. But if you have goals written you can always pick up where you left off in your planning.

Goals are rules you make for yourself and must not be broken. I have my own rules about my goals. I DO NOT DO UNREALISTIC GOALS, I'm not saying don't set unrealistic goals, but only set goals that you have power over and you can achieve! For instance, I walk/run maybe 3 to 4 times a week. At the beginning of the week or even at night before bed I will write my goals for the next day. If it is not written down, it's not something I'm expected to do. But what also helps me, if I have then written and don't view them that day, it really bothers. It makes me feel like I've worked on everyone else goals and left mine behind. This means that I've had a setback for that day. Even when writing this book, if I am not consistent with writing, before you know it… it will be weeks later and nothing done towards my goals.

My best friend told me one day that we were supposed to go walking every day, I told him that this was not written in my goals book, so it didn't count. My rules are if I write it I must do it. See there are so many ways you can be creative and set your own goals and rules. There are no rules to how goals are met. One thing that I've learned as I write this book, and that's everytime I read a chapter from the day before I start adding more to that chapter. I realized that if you start out with unrealistic goals, then your goals will be bigger than your dreams. This may work for some. I advise anyone to know your limits, some people don't have limits, and that's great, but in making goals make sure your limits are within the time you have set for your business.

Keywords to your mobile boutique/fashion truck goals:
• Building platform
• Define, (license, Insurance state laws)
• Identifying: recognize your ability to make this work
• List: many connected items or names that can help build your platform
• Name: giving your boutique the most unique name you can think of.
• Recall: write every detailed information you've gathered.
• Recognize: acknowledge the existence you've put together for your boutique (get excited).
• Record: keep record of every piece of information and ideas you've collected.
• Relate: show connection and communication to every source.

• Repeat: if it takes repeatedly times to get something done, please by all means keep doing it.

• Underline: key items and source that will help you build a successful business.

• Location: I know you've heard this before" location is key" make sure your location is in a high traffic area.

• Merchandise: Don't spend money buying merchandise until you are 110% sure what you will market.

• Schedule: work on your business plans at least 1 to 3 hours a day. I blocked 2 hours a day but most of the times I'll go over.

Deadlines: are very important, you should always have deadlines in place. This was one of the hardest thing for me to keep up with! Some deadlines were because of my planning conflict, but most of them were situations I could not help. So, when planning and setting goals always allow yourself more time than planned. It will keep you from getting discouraged and frustrated if you don't meet your deadline.

My Goals Worksheet

My _______ Year Goal

Goal:____ (Specific,
Measurable, Authentic, Realistic, Timely and Inspiring)

It is important I achieve this goal because:
____
____
____

Steps I Must Take to Achieve My Goal:
1.
2.
3.
4.
5.
6.
7.
The skills and knowledge I need to be successful:
____
____
____

How will I know when I have achieved success
____
____

The quote that inspires me to stay motivated
____
____
____
____
____

Chapter 2: The Idea

I stated earlier than it took me years to start my business, well it all didn't just come to me overnight. I had an idea and I peddled that idea until I had sores on my feet. (a little humor).

The first thing you want to do is gather all of your ideas and put them on paper. Every time something comes to your mind, write it down. Some things that sweep through your mind will be questionable to you, like... "this is stupid", but "NO" "DO NOT THROW IT OUT JUST YET" Write it on paper! Collect all of your ideas, once your paper is full of ideas,start building your platform from that one sheet. Once that's done, start another sheet of paper until that's full. Before you know it, you will have all of your ideas together. You will be on your way to starting your business. Don't be afraid to change some things on your paper, somethings are not meant to go along with you!

You will notice that once you start writing, everything will start to form the shape of a circle. Make sure you keep everything in that circle.
The circle of ideas will capture and store all your bright ideas.

Remember these are the techniques I used to start my business, you may want to use a different concept. I choose a circle because nothing can break the circle. The more ideas you have the larger your circle will be.

When doing your research, the most important thing is to find out the laws for food trucks and mobile boutiques in your state. I suggest that you go in person and visit your local official offices. You will be surprised by what you may find out about starting your own mobile business. I remember when I first thought about opening my business, I thought to myself wow this is a lot to do! Then it came to me, how is it a lot if this is your passion?

I started reading laws and asking questions in my state and city. I got lots of handouts and highlight. Most of what was beneficial to me. I cut and paste it on my vision board.

Another important tip, some cities won't allow fashion trucks in certain areas of the city. This is also something you would want to find out before you make any other location decisions.

After all of your paperwork has been collected, if you haven't already came up with a name. You want to think about a name for your business. It is always good to do a google search, or go to the secretary of state website and enter in your business name. If the name is taken it will be in their database.

If the name is not taken, you want to get the name registered immediately and file for a EIN number on the IRS website.

The EIN number is free, but to file with the secretary of state office it is a fee. The fee varies from state to state. Having the name registered and having the EIN number, this will make you feel like you've accomplished a lot, but make sure you stay focused and stick to your goals. This is just the beginning of your process. You still have a way to go.

Don't stop the process! Once you stop your process, it's very hard to pick up where you left off!! Ask me how I know so well!

My Idea Brainstorming Worksheet

The number one reason that I want to start a mobile boutique is:
____

Some of my other business ideas are:
____
____
____
____
____
____

The top 5 problems that I want to help people solve are:
____
____
____
____
____ The top 5 pain points I think people have are:
____
____
____
____
____

My top 5 problems are:

____

____

____

____

____

Next Step: Create or find marketable solutions the the problems and pain points mentioned above. Go through each item you listed above and….well….Google it! See what (or who) is already out there. If products already exist, can you create a competing product that approaches the solution in a faster, simpler or even cheaper way? Or maybe instead of a competing product, you can create a complimentary product that can sell alongside the products already on the market. The ideas here is to brainstorm each thought that came to your mind and explore their profitability .

Chapter 3: The Startup

First thing's first, you will first need to determine what kind of business you would want to open! Let's compare price for a moment. First off starting a mobile boutique will cost thousands of dollars less than a brick and mortar. The term brick and mortar were an unknown language when I first started my business. So, for those of you who don't know what a brick and mortar is, here you go!

A **Brick and Mortar** (also **brick and mortar** or B&M) refers to a physical presence of an **organization** or **business** in a building or other structure. The term **brick and mortar business** are often used to refer to a **company** that possesses or leases retail stores, factory production facilities, or warehouses for its **operations**. The start up cost for a brick and mortar can be from $25,000 to $450,000. What a piggy bank breaker!!! In doing my research and talking to business owners, most said it would be easier and cheapest to get a mobile store on wheels. I didn't know so many local business owners considered moving their business to a mobile business, also setting up a pop-up shop in business parks.

Determining if you want a brick and mortar or mobile store is solely up to you, but for me the start-up cost was amazingly the best move for me. I didn't want the headache of all the extra overhead cost. Overhead cost like building maintenance, electricity, water, lease, employees, security, phone etc. Having a trailer would be so much easier to handle.

Box Truck vs Cargo Trailer
The decision is solely up to you, but… what I will do is talk about other "Fashion Truck" owner experiences.

I've heard "Fashion Truck" owners talk about finding the right truck. Most of the used box trucks come with high mileage unless you plan to purchase a new box truck. Most of them are bring use as package or bread trucks driving all around the city. Some of them from state to state. Some of them are not treated with care, most of the time if it's not yours, you tend to mistreat or shall I say mishandled when driving. Some companies also don't keep up with mechanical maintenance on these box trucks. It's just a few things to think about.

If your box truck goes down and you have an upcoming show, this can also be stressful. I'm not trying to discourage you on your purchase, but wanted to share my experience and opinion. These are some of the things you want to consider. However ; if you are married to a mechanic or have one in your family having options can be great. Trying to pay for mechanical maintenance, stocking merchandise for a show,and the cost of getting to a show (fuel, parking, food) could also be stressful, and of course break your piggy bank!
Let's talk about the cargo trailer!

Yes, having ownership of a cargo can also be costly, but the overhead mechanical maintenance is not too bad. The most you would have to worry about is having a reliable, heavy duty equip vehicle to pull your cargo. Logically speaking; if you are having a show, or on schedule to set up at an event, if something happens to your vehicle right before a show, it is always easier to rent a vehicle that will accommodate your cargo. Sure, other things could also go wrong, like a flat tire on your cargo, but for the most part for me having a cargo is much easier and less expensive than a box truck.

Let the decision be yours, you are the only person who knows how things will work out if you find yourself in one of these situations.

One of the most challenging things for me is parking the cargo! When signing up for a show, if you are going to sell out of your boutique, please let the event planner know that you a traveling with a cargo trailer. You may have to reserve two spaces.

Take some time to learn how to drive, back and park the cargo! This is a must if you don't already know! The biggest cost for my boutique was setting it up like a store. Well the floor plan was more of a challenge. So here I am dealing with a 6x17 box that I had to make look like a boutique. This was really the fun part. We spent at least $5000 trying to build out the box. We went with 3 different plans for the boutique. I thought about having it black and white with old fashion looking newspaper on the walls.

We took a weekend trip to Charleston, South Carolina as a business planning trip. We love that place, so finding reasons to go there is always fun. Well while we were there , we were looking at designs online for our boutique. We saw a black and white design with old sandy looking newspaper. I youtubed how to make newspaper look old and worn out. Someone had a video where they had unsweet tea and sprayed the newspaper. Once the newspaper dried, it would have that nice old fashion look. Well I decided that I wanted to buy as many newspapers as possible from Charleston SC and that's what I did.

Then I came up with this bright idea, to buy a large stapler and staple the newspaper to the he walls of the boutique. We bought a spray bottle and went to work. It wasn't looking as attractive as I thought it would. I was worried about asking my friend to let's take it down and try painting. He was such a trooper, he agreed to helping me remove the newspaper and each staple out of the wall. It took us just as long to take all of that down as it took us putting it up.
We decided to paint it black and white instead. So, he went out and bought 3 gallons of paint in each color. We started painting. It looked amazingly great after we were done with the black and white paint. I thought it would be different and look nice if the floors were black as well.

The outcome was looking great. The next thing was trying to get the perfect furniture for the boutique. I wanted an old fashion look. We went to Goodwill and purchase old furniture and painted then multi-color. Things still wasn't looking the way I imagined it.

One day I was sitting at my desk and decided to look on craigslist for some unique furniture, well I saw something better. A local department store was going out of business, and had almost all their displays on sale. We went and found 3 large pieces of displays, and a large picture of a lady shopping. This was the ideal setup, so we purchased the items.

They were heavy and bulky but was becoming of the boutique. We went through 2 floor plans before we decided to go with the displays. Well the downfall about the displays where they were not mount, so every time we drove we had to lay everything down. Once we reached our destination we had to setup the boutique. It was time consuming and tiring. It was taking us just as much time setting up to sell than actually selling. Please always and I do mean always, have extra hard-working hands tagging alone with you. I call them laborers!

If allowed by the event planner I always arrive at least 3 hours ahead before the show starts. This will allow some play time just in case something does not work out, or maybe you accidently left an important factor behind. Plus being set up and on time says a lot about your business.

I then decided that I wanted to get some manikins. My daughter went to the mall one day and saw where this store was going out of business. She called me and said that the store was selling manikins. I bought two full size pink manikins for $100.00 each. I thought this was a great deal because they are full size, standing, pink mannequin. They look great with pearls and other accessories.

Remember that this is your race and your pace, don't get overwhelmed while planning and setting up. I spoke to a few "Fashion Truck" owners and they said building out was one of the hardest thing. Mostly because you will never know how it's going to work if you don't try it. Plus, trying gives you the opportunity to see if you will like the set up. Trust me before this is all over…. you will transform your boutique so many times, especially if you're a creative person. Creativity can be an amazing thing!

My start up financially wasn't bad. I worked a second job, used all of that money to build my business. This is something you may want to consider or seek financial advice from a financial adviser. My goal was to not use bank loans or credit cards to start my business. This is just another bill, plus I'm claiming and working on debt free for my future. Everything I own for my business is mine. I did not want to work a business to pay for the business. I wanted to work my business and save my profits.

My Business Research Worksheet

1. The reasons for choosing a mobile boutique are:

____

____

____

____

2. The name of my boutique will be______________
3. I will have a list of fixtures, racks, displays, mannequins that my boutique will need by __/__/____ .
4. The exterior color of my mobile boutique will be________________________.

5. The type of trailer/camper I will use for my mobile boutique will be: (manufacturer, length etc)

____

____

____

6. The vehicle that I will use to pull my mobile boutique will be:

____

7. The categories of items that I will sell from my mobile boutique will be (accessories, clothing, cosmetics etc):____

8. The date my mobile boutique will be ready to open is ____/___/___.
9. The method I will use to get my first client is (advertising):________________________

Chapter 4: Networking

Business networking is leveraging your **business,** and personal connections to bring you a regular supply of new **business**. The concept sounds simple, doesn't it?

Don't let that fool you! It involves relationship building, it can be a deceptively complex process. Think about it. How many ...Networking does it take to interact with other?

Networking requires you being an outgoing person. This was somewhat hard for me because I don't consider myself as an outgoing person. It also requires you to be a great salesperson. I had to learn how to get together with business owners and also joined business groups on social media. For the most part I try networking wherever I go.

Networking is like linking chains together, the more links you have the longer your chain will be. Well same with networking, the more people and resources you link with , the more people will hear about you and the greater your business will grow.

When I started networking, I joined facebook and created a business account, I invited my personal page of friends to like my business page. I've also created a separate account for other entrepreneurs to also link. Facebook also offers ads to business owners for a small fee.

There's also Twitter and Instagram just to mention a few. Making sure you have a target audience of people who will support you. On social media I have family, friends, business owners and just random people I don't know. I don't expect to get rich from my social media audience unless I'm doing what it takes to get their attention.

Most of my sales have been from my online store, and referrals, but the biggest success comes from my private home parties. My private home parties bring in more than any other vendor I've done. Home parties are also a great networking resource.
Discounts: giving discounts can also give you more leverage to grow, this will get your customers interested in shopping with you on a regular.

Promotions: Running promotional ads and giveaways on special occasions, holidays etc.

Offering free shipping: Offer free shipping on orders over an amount of cash value.

Referrals: Offer a discount for each referral, this will also help build your business.

Live shopping: Social media has made it possible for us to go live, this is a great tool to use to have fashion shows of your merchandise or just a showcase live.

When going live, make sure you have your items numbered and let your audience know to inbox you with their interest. A great way to keep up with the response is to have someone help by checking your inbox while you continue to do your shows live. This is a great way to make money.

My Vendor/Contact List

Top 5 mobile boutique owners who I would like to connect with:

Name_____________________________website____________

Email_______________________

other contact method_____________________

Name_____________________________website____________

Email_______________________

other contact method_____________________

Name_____________________________website____________

Email_______________________

other contact method_____________________

Name_____________________________website____________

Email_______________________

other contact method_____________________

Top 5 websites that I will source my products from:

Store

Name_____________________________Website__________

Store

Name_________________________________Website___________
Store
Name_________________________________Website___________
Store
Name_________________________________Website___________
Store
Name_________________________________Website___________
Contact list from previous shows

Name
____________________________phone_______________ show date___________

Name
____________________________phone_______________ show date___________

Name
____________________________phone_______________ show date___________

Name
____________________________phone_______________ show date___________

Name
____________________________phone_______________ show date___________

Name
____________________________phone_______________ show date___________
Name
____________________________phone_______________ show date___________

Name
____________________________phone_______________ show date___________

Name
____________________________phone_______________ show date___________

Name
____________________________phone_______________ show date___________

Mobile Boutique Tow Vehicle
mechanic________________________________
Tow Company (in case of
breakdown)______________________________

Chapter 5: Building Your Website

I believe every business owner should have a presence on the internet. Bill
Gates said "If your business is not on the internet, then your business will be
out of business." This is especially true for mobile businesses. Simply put,
your need somewhere where you can always be found. Almost every soul in
the world has been conditioned to look to the internet for whatever it is they
want. Even if you have a brick and mortar store, people will go to the internet
to see your hours of operation so it would serve you well to have a website
for your mobile boutique business.

When building your website, start out with a testimony, explain how you got
started , make your story interesting. Share what made you wanted to start
your own business, what drove you to just step out? Who motivated you to
get started? All of this should be on the cover of you website with a very
interesting picture of you.

Your logo should also be included on your website as well, make your tabs
easy access, by including everything you think would help your business.
Every time I have a show, I always post my pictures on my website, after all;
it is your website so you have the ability to add and subtract as much as you
want.

Building a website can be very expensive, one way how you can save money
is find someone who build websites as a secondary income, or simply just for
fun. Thank God my best friend knew how to build websites and he taught me
how to keep it up.

All websites and Web Hosting Services are not created equal. You want to
know what type of web presence you want and what your content will be
about before you spend one penny on a domain name and web hosting.

From the minute you buy your domain name, the clock starts ticking and 365 days later, you will have to renew your domain name (pay for using it for another year). In order to maximize every dollar you invest in your business, you want to take advantage of every "free" opportunity you can. When I got started online, I rushed out and got a website set up. Then time went by as I then tried to figure out just what I was going to do with this brand new site. I thought it was a great accomplishment to finally have a website of my own but with no plan and no vision, I was really wasting money as the days ticked by and I went to bed night after night with no progress on my site. You won't make that mistake because you've already done a ton of research "off the clock".

Now it's time to zero in on your domain name. Before you choose your name there are 2 things you need to take into consideration; one is how the search engines will view your site and two is how your visitors will view your site.

As cool and as interesting a person as you probably are, the search engines just don't care. The only thing the search engines care about is matching the best result to the search term entered in the search box.

For this reason, you should consider having your niche somewhere in your domain name. The reason for this is that it will give you an advantage in the search engines (if you are a newbie, you want all the advantages you can get).

If my subject was dogs and my niche was Cocker Spaniels, I might try to get the term "cocker spaniel" somewhere in my domain name (you actually want your domain name to begin with this term.

Now I could try cockerspaniels.com but that's already taken.

A creative way around this is to add a suffix to "cocker spaniel" such as cockerspanielworld.com or cockerspanieluniverse.com. This would give you the relevant term "cocker spaniel" while at the same time separating you from the other websites with the same term.

Both of the above examples will also give your potential visitors a general idea of what your site is about. I could have separated each word with dashes, but I have a couple of sites with dashes in the domain name. But let me tell you, I think it's harder to get them ranked than domain names without dashes.

I don't know why but that's my experience.

You may have seen websites or blogs that don't have the niche or subject in the domain name. These are sites where the owner may have used his or her own name as the domain name but their content could be another subject entirely. This is OK when you are building an authority site (a site that will cover every aspect of a given niche).

When I started out, I definitely used the search term in my domain name and if you are starting out, I recommend you do the same.

It's really up to you but some things you want to think about before you choose a domain name are:

1. Will this name still be relevant in a year? Choosing a domain name like funniestmomentsof2013.com would be outdated in about (yep…you guessed it) 12 months tops.

2. Is this a topic I can create content for over a long period of time?
3. Is the domain name short enough for a stranger to remember?

The reason you want to ask all these questions up front is because once you buy a domain name, it cannot be changed. You are stuck with it for at least a year.

To see if your domain name ideas are available click here namecheap.com
Will you build a blog or a website?

The difference between a blog and a website is that a blog has it's entries in a chronological order and each entry (otherwise called a page or a post) is listed with the newest entry at the top of your homepage and the older ones towards the bottom.

The benefit of this is that a blog is easier to keep updated than a static (the front page never changes) website. For a static website, you would have to redo your front page in order to get any significant changes. This is not necessary as it's quite easy to just add an extra page to your site.

Another benefit of a blog over a website is that your readers don't have to work as hard to keep up with your latest content. This is huge when trying to get people to know, like and trust you! Anytime you make that process easier, you benefit by getting more people to "stick" to your content and brand.

Of course you know by now that I recommend a blog over a static website. You can always build both and see which works best for you.

If you chose to build a static website, you should consider creating a sniper site. This is a small website (4-10 pages) that focuses on one aspect of a niche. For example; I might build a sniper site dealing with just potty training Cocker Spaniels. The whole site will deal with just that topic and nothing else.

The benefit of this is that it would be much easier to get this site to rank highly in the search engines because you would be viewed as having a ton of targeted information on this narrow subject. While most people would be mentioning potty training or they may even commit a page or two about the subject, you would have an entire website committed to this small subject. You would also have the keyphrase "potty training" in your domain name.

That aspect alone would give you incredible leverage in the search engines when competing with other sites that merely list potty training as a page extension off the main site.

Here's an example:

Cockerspanielpottytraining.com would get way more traction in the search engines than wonderfulcockerspaniels.com/potty-training-your-cocker/.

The only downside is that your very focused domain name would force you to devote this entire site to this topic only (which is the point).

There are many marketers who go the sniper site route. They would just create many sites like this.
Where did the term "sniper site" come from?

It came from one of my mentors, George Brown. This young man(I'm more than 10 years older than he is) is absolutely one of the best teachers I have ever had. To see the program that got me started, go to George Brown on Sniper Sites.

Today's Assignment:
Today's assignment is to pick out and purchase your domain name. The cost shouldn't be over $15 per year.

I recommend going with namecheap.com they are very easy to work with and super simple to set up. I will be using them in the tutorial so if you are using them too, it will be easier to follow along.

You also have the option of buying your domain name from the same company you get your hosting from.

I keep all my domain name purchases separate from my hosting purchases because when you get everything from one place, they will try to lock you into certain packages. You may not need that particular website you're working on. I also may have websites set up on different hosting platforms and keeping my domain names separate, means I don't have to renew the domain name and the host at the end of the year. If I wanted to renew my domain name but move it to a different web host, I could easily do it. Just a thought.
Now we are going to set up your website or blog using what I call the QFR Principle. We have a lot to do today so don't be concerned if this takes you more than one actual day to do.

QFR stands for:
Quality
Findability
Relevance

Quality
Because of the competitive nature of the online marketplace, you simply cannot afford a poor quality work ethic. In addition, your visitors deserve the highest quality content available and you should make a commitment to give it to them. In order to focus on quality the way you really should, you have to

place earning money online behind providing value for your visitors. It may feel funny at first to "give" anything first before you get any money in return but quality must be first or you won't make any money at all. Insist on doing everything in a first class manner and you will definitely be rewarded.

Findability

All the high quality information in the world won't do you any good if you can't be found online. That's right, I'm talking about getting traffic. The whole "if you make it, they will come" only works in the movies. You have to either "drive" (buy) or attract (free search engine traffic) visitors to your site.

The first step in this process is making sure every detail of your site is SEO'd (search engine optimized) so that the search engines "understand" what your site is about and ranks it accordingly.

Relevance

Nothing is more frustrating to click through to a website only to be met by all the information in the world…except what you're looking for. If someone is searching for information, they are not looking for a sales pitch. Even though you may know of a product that could help solve a problem your visitor may be looking for an answer to, you have to first give them the information they are looking for and then "pre-sell" them on the product you are offering.

Slam your visitors with ad after ad when they visit your site and they will click away faster than you can blink.

Everything we will discuss in this chapter will center around the QFR Principle. Basically, if it doesn't add a high level of quality, help your blog to be found or if it's not relevant to your blog's content and mission; we won't do it.

OK so with this in mind, let's go set up your site!

Setting up your site will require 3 main components: A Domain Name, Web Hosting and a Content Management System.

Domain Names

I've already given you my thoughts on where to get a domain name from (namecheap.com). I will be using namecheap in this tutorial but the process is similar for any domain registrar. For me, it's not the purchasing process through namecheap that keeps me going back. No, it's easy after the sale and that's why I keep going back. I have tried godaddy.com and the relationship after the sale leaves a lot to be desired. Just a personal opinion that's all.

Web Hosting

A web host is a company that will actually store your website content on their computer (servers). It goes without saying that the more reliable your web hosting company is, the more reliable your website will be. Every time your web host has technical difficulties, your website stands a greater chance of having difficulties. All web hosts are not created equal.
This is one reason I don't recommend setting up a free website. Nine times out of ten, you will get burned or your business will be handicapped by the limitations of your hosting company. You just don't want that. Plus, since it costs less than $20 per month to get stellar web hosting, why not?

I must say though that my very first experience with a website was with Blogger.com. This is actually a free service owned by Google. Blogger is great for information and some of the linking strategies I will mention later but you don't want a blogger.com blog to start a life-sustaining website.

I recommend Hostgator.com for your web hosting. Their Business Plan (the mid-level plan) is the best for beginners because with one hosting account, you can set up several websites. They say you can set up "unlimited" domains but that's not quite true. I would stick to 20 sniper sites or 4 authority sites per Business Plan.

I have had websites with Hostgator, Bluehost and also with SiteBuildit!(more on them later) and by far, it was easier to get up and running with Hostgator. Right now I can literally have another website up and running within minutes.

Content Management System

A Content Management System is a program that organizes your site so that it's readable by people. Facebook wouldn't exist without a content management system. Yahoo wouldn't be Yahoo without a content management system. When you log into a yahoo, gmail (or any other familiar service like these), you use their content management system to do it. When you leave a comment on facebook, you are using their content management system to do it.

In my opinion, the best content management system out there today is **Wordpress**. Not only is it super easy to use but it is the most popular. It is also free with your webhosting account (all content management systems are free to my knowledge). I have the vast majority of my experience with Wordpress so that's what we'll be using today.

A Word About Sitebuildit! By Sitesell

Sitebuidit!(now called Solobuildit!) Is an all-in-one service whereby you can learn all about setting up a dynamite website (they have a 10 day video tutorial that really breaks every aspect of online marketing down so that a 5th grader could understand), get your domain name and also there's a built in content management system. They even have tons of research tools so that you never need to leave their platform for anything. The scope of this book is centered around Namecheap.com (domain names), Hostgator.com (web hosting) and Wordpress (content management system) so we won't go into detail about Sitebuildit! Here.

You may be asking "If Sitebuildit! Is so great, why don't you just use that and forget about everyone else?"

Sitebuildit! Is great if you are only going to build one site. Over the years, I have developed several sites. With Sitebuildit!, the price never changes. When you buy your first site ($29 per month) you get access to all the great tutorials, research tools and coaching about how to get started. That $29 seems really worth it. The problem is that every site after your first one is also $29/month. Once you've learned all there is to learn, it seems like you're paying for an education program that you've already graduated from.

A word of caution though; if you do get a website through Sitesell, **don't** buy your domain name first! Be sure to buy it through them or else you will have to wait 30 days for your domain name to transfer to their service (ouch!). When going through the video tutorials, the domain name purchase part comes in Day 5 of their program. That way will show you cost less and you will only purchase what you need and nothing you don't. :) **Let's Get Started Setting Up Your Blog:**

Section 1: Installing & Optimizing Your Blog

Step 1 - If you haven't already secured your domain name, go ahead and do that now. To do that, go to
namecheap.com

Once there, enter the domain name idea and click the search button.

When the results come back, you only want the ".com" version of the name if it's available. Don't get discouraged if your name idea isn't available.

Remember to get creative and add letters or words to the end of your name idea so that you still get the Google Juice from the keyphrase and it's unique enough that nobody else has it.

Once that's done, go on and purchase the domain name (if it costs more than $15, choose another name). To purchase through namecheap.com, you will Need to set up an account with them. This is where you will keep track of all your domain names over time. OK, keep your namecheap account login information handy and let's go on to step 2.

Step 2- Go to Hostgator.com and click on "View Web Hosting Plans".

Once you've done that, you want to purchase their "**Business Plan**". The reason for this is that you want the benefit of a private IP address.

Why should you want a private IP? Well when Google penalizes a website, all the websites on the same IP could potentially be affected. This Google Penalty is called the "Google Slap" and it mainly happens to websites with poor quality content and poor quality backlinks. This is the reason why you Don't want free hosting and you don't want the "entry level" paid hosting account. The good news is that it doesn't cost much more to upgrade.

Trust me, you don't want to skimp on this area. You may find that no matter how good you build your website, it may still struggle from too many other spammy websites on the same IP address. From time to time, Hostgator will offer discounts on signing up.

Be sure that you **do not** purchase your domain name through hostgator. Hostgator will then send you an email with all of your login and name server information.

Your name servers in your email will look like this:
-ns.xxxx.hostgator.com
-ns.xxxx.hostgator.com
(x represents numerical characters. I have mine hidden for security purposes)
*You will need both of them to point your hosting account to your domain name.

What you are going to do is copy and paste these name servers into your namecheap account. This is what will connect your hosting service to your domain Name.

Now log into your namecheap account.
Now click on the "my account" button in the top right corner of the page:
Now click on "manage domains".
At this point, click on the domain name you just purchased

Now on the left side of the page, you should see a tab called "transfer DNS to webhost". Click that. Now in the middle of the page, select the "specify custom DNS servers".

Now in box 1 you want to paste the 1st nameserver there (an example would be "ns.1234.hostgator.com"). Make sure there are no spaces before or after.

Then in box 2 you want to paste the 2nd nameserver there (an example would be "ns.1235.hostgator.com").
Now click "save changes" at the bottom.

It will take a few moments to transfer and you have successfully connected your domain name to your webhosting account.

In the next step, you will set up your domain on your hosting account (turn it into a website you can recognize).

Step 3 - In your web browser, enter your domain name followed by /cpanel. Yourdomainname.com/cpanel

This is where you would enter the username and password emailed to you at set up.
Now we will set up your email. It's very important that you learn to do business from your business email address. It's more professional and it also promotes your website (you'll actually get more traffic).

Scroll down to the "mail" section and click on "email accounts".

Once you've clicked on that, you will need to set up the actual email. I recommend you use an email like admin@yourdomain.com or info@yourdomain.com. If you want to add a personal touch (this is what I do with my sites) you could use yourname@yourdomain.com.

Go ahead and create a password for your email account. Be sure to select the "unlimited" email quota box. Now click "create account".

To access your email, select the "more" tab in the "Actions" section and click "access webmail" from the drop down box. It is a good idea to make your email easy to reach by pinning it to your web browser.

This way, I can access my email without having to login to a thousand different accounts first:).
Now go back to your cpanel and let's set up wordpress…
Click on the "wordpress" button on the left side of the page:
Now click "**new installation**".

When you do this you will need to select your domain name from the drop down menu. This tells hostgator which domain to install wordpress on.

Don't put anything in the box labeled "**install in directory**"

Under **Admin Access Data**, create a new username and password. This is the username and password you will use to login to the dashboard of your website. Be sure to store this in a place that you can easily get to until you memorize it. Your computer should remember this information after the first time you log in but You should be able to access it quickly.

Be sure to use either a pen name or your real name as your **Admin Nickname**. If you use something like "funlover123", people will see that name when you make posts and entries into your Blog. A pen name or your real name would seem more professional.

For the **Site name**, enter your domain name here.

The **description** box is where your site's catch phrase will go. This should be about 1 short sentence describing the essence of your website. Both your site name
and your description will appear in the header of your website.

Once you are finished, click **"Install Wordpress"**.

To get to the dashboard of your website, enter your domain name in your web browser followed by /wp-admin. It would look like this:
Yourdomainname.com/wp-admin

You should be asked to enter your username and password. This is the same username and password you entered for the Admin Access Data section when you Set up wordpress.

In the next step we will configure your website so that you can start making post entries.
Step 4-Configuring your Wordpress Blog
A. Theme Selection

Now that you've logged into your WP-Admin (dashboard), the first thing you want to do is set up your theme. The basic Wordpress default theme is actually a good one because it is basic and not very flashy. When doing business online, simple is best and it sells better. Keep it as basic as possible.

What simplicity does is it allows your readers to spot your content more easily, helps your pages load faster and gives your overall perception one of cleanliness and organization. People who will be searching for your content are the type to be put off by flashing lights, audio that starts automatically when they click on a page etc. If you want to make money online, don't have a flashy, loud site.

Wordpress has a ton of free themes that will suit your purpose just fine.
To browse through the free themes, click on "appearance" (located on the left column of your dashboard)
Next, select the "themes" tab. Now, click on the "install themes" tab at the top:

At this point, you can browse through hundreds of themes until you find one that suits you. Remember to keep it simple and try not to get overwhelmed. You can always change themes later if you happen to choose one and then realize you don't like it.

In order to find these themes, just enter the theme name in the search box.

Once you find a theme you like, click "install now" beneath the theme and then click "activate". Your new theme will be set up.

B. Change The Permalinks
Click on "Settings", then click on "permalinks"
Select the "custom structure" settings and enter /%postname%/ in the field next to it.
Now click "save changes".

What this does is create search engine friendly urls when you create pages and posts. Now your url will display the post title next to the main url instead of a bunch of numbers and other foreign characters that won't help your search engine rankings a bit.

Your site will go from looking like this: yourdomain.com/123?33
To this: yourdomain.com/postname (whatever title you gave a particular post)

Now it's time to create your first post. The first one should be a welcome post. It won't be very long but it will serve as a beginning to what will be a very profitable blog.

To do this, go to your dashboard and click on "posts".
Now click on "add new".

The title area is where you will put the title of your post and in the body area, you should write a brief introduction to your blog and tell people what they can expect in the future. Once this is done, click publish on the right side of the page.

Now on the left side of your dashboard, click on "Settings" and then click on "reading" and you should see this page: This is where you decide whether or not you will have a static website or a blog. Wordpress, by default, is set up as a blog. Leave it that way. If you wanted to create a static home page then you would check the appropriate box (you may choose to do this with some of your sites).

At any time, if you wanted to see how your blog looks live, just hover your mouse over the sites name located right above the dashboard menu on the top left. A menu will appear and then you should click on "visit site".

C- Configure The Widgets

This is an area where there are no hard and fast rule. Widget is basically a content holder that will be placed in the sidebar of your blog. Usually the widgets will be placed on the right sidebar but some people have them on the left sidebar. To keep things simple, just keep them on the right.

To get to your widgets, go to your dashboard and click on "appearance", then click on "widgets".

You can drag and drop the widgets from the "available widgets" over to the main sidebar. You will notice that when you drag an individual widget over, you can place it above or below any other widget so that keeping them in the order you want is a snap. I recommend setting them up like you see in the above illustration at least for now. This will give you a basic, functional setup that you can modify later as your experience grows and your needs change.

Be careful with the "search" widget. Some themes already come with a search box installed. If you drag a search widget over, you will essentially be displaying 2 search boxes on your site….not cool.

The search widget will allow people to search your blog.

The recent posts widget will show the latest posts on the right side of your blog while your current post will occupy the main real estate in the center of your blog.

The categories widget will allow your visitors to view your posts that you have grouped together according to various subjects.

Your archive widget will display your posts according to month and year.
D- Key Plugins

Wordpress can be enhanced by an awesome array of plugins. There are free plugins and there are also premium plugins (paid). The plugins we will install today are free and they will work wonders for your blog.

Right now, there are 2 plugins we need to install on your blog:
1. All in one SEO pack- Will help keep your blog optimized for the search engines.

2. Wordpress SEO- Creates a map that Google can follow when it's spiders visit your site. This is another SEO weapon that will help boost your blog in the
Search engine rankings.

Go back to your dashboard and click on "plugins". Now click on "add new"
Type each plugin into the search box one at a time.
On the next page, click on "install now" beside the desired plugin. Then click "activate plugin"
Now that you've installed your plugins, it's time to configure them.
All in one SEO pack configuration.
Click on "settings" from your dashboard and then click "all in one seo".
Be sure to fill in the fields as I have outlined below and then leave the rest as is:

Wordpress SEO Configuration
From your dashboard, click on "SEO" and then click on "xml sitemaps".
Check the box to enable sitemap functionality.

This plugin will automatically tell Google and Bing when you have fresh
content (pinging). Go ahead and check the boxes that ask it to also ping
yahoo.com and Ask.com. Yahoo.com and Bing are currently operating
together using the Bing search engine but check this box anyway. Leave the
rest at the default settings.

For now, we will leave the rest of the plugin configuration alone. You can
come back and modify the rest of this configuration as your experience
grows. The reason you don't want a cookie cutter setting is because different
blogs will have different needs where this configuration is concerned.

When you are building posts and pages, these plugins will also give you great
suggestions on optimizing your page before the page goes live. We'll see
more on this later.

Believe me, there are tons of modifications that you can make to your blog
but don't worry, Wordpress comes pretty well set up out of the box other than
what I've just shown you. As you grow your online business, you will learn
what your blog needs more or less of and you will also learn to make changes
accordingly.

Another great plugin you may want to look into to help your pages load faster
is **W3 Total Cache.**
E. The 4 Essential Pages
There are 4 essential pages you will need to ad to your blog. They are:
1. A Privacy Policy
2. An Affiliate Disclaimer
3. An About Us Page 4. A Contact Us Page
Each of these is critical to your blog.

I am not a lawyer so I will not tell you how to set up your privacy policy but
you need to research it and add one to your blog. It needs to be a page and not
a post. You can add it to the footer, header or sidebar but you must have one.
If you don't, you could face some legal issues down the road.

I can tell you that Wordpress has a free plugin that you can add to your site
called Easy Privacy Plugin.
All you have to do to add any plugin to your Wordpress blog is follow these
7 steps:

1. Download the plugin to your computer. I always send it to my desktop so
that it's in easy reach.
2. Click on "plugins" from your blog's dashboard.
3. Click on "add new"
4. Click on "upload" at the top of the screen
5. Select the desired plugin from the place you downloaded it on your
computer
6. Once you get a message saying it has been successfully installed, activate
it.
7. You may have to then go into the plugin and set it up the way you want it.
Next we will begin adding content to your blog.

Section 2- Building Your Blog For Performance, Power and Profits
3 Essential Pages
In this next section I will show you how to:
1. "Season" your blog
2. Add your picture to the sidebar

1. Seasoning Your Blog & Search Engine Optimize Your Content
With all the updates that Google is making to it's algorithms, you will need to
use thought and caution to everything you post to the web. Before we start
throwing up a bunch of affiliate links, Adsense and the like, we need to be
mindful of how you go about this or all your efforts may actually hurt your
blog and not help it.

Our process will be really simple. No shortcuts! This is an area where
thousands of potentially stellar bloggers fail. Motivated by fast money, quick
results and the desire to see progress NOW, many people resort to buying
backlinks, spinning articles to the point that they aren't readable by humans
etc. Google has picked up on thi because it has started to affect their main
product....search results.

I don't have to tell you that if you use Google to search for information and the only results you get are ads, ads, more ads, content that looks like a drunken monkey typed it etc., you would probably either stop using that search engine or…go to the library to find your information. In order to keep it's search results of the highest quality, Google is weeding out all the spamy, money grabbing blogs and sites out there and making them impossible to be found in the search results.

This won't happen to your blog because you will insist on only the highest quality content. You will offer valuable information first and only then will you follow up with products that further enhance the visitor's experience. Planning on writing articles? Be sure to make them as close to 100% unique as possible. Spun articles are going the way of the dodo bird.

The first thing you need to do now is season your blog. This is a process where you create 8-10 high quality posts and let them age for 2-3 weeks before you try to monetize. These posts should not contain affiliate links or Google Adsense. Once you have done this, then you can begin to introduce posts that have Adsense and affiliate links on them.
This and anything else you can do to tell Google that your priority is valuable content first will help you obtain and keep the rankings you deserve.

2. Adding Your Picture To The Sidebar
Doing business online is mostly a matter of trust. It takes the average visitor seven visits to your site before they will buy anything. The reason for this has to do with many factors. Without a face to face transaction, you have to overcome the visitors fears of getting ripped off and not being able to do anything about it. They will also want to know who is behind the "curtain". If you put up a site and hide your identity or make it hard to get to know you in any way at all, you will make fewer sales.

The remedy for this is to put yourself out there from the beginning. Actually, once a sale is made, people are "buying" into you as much as they are the product you are offering. So don't be afraid to put a face to the brand.

One great way to do this is to put a picture of yourself in your blog's sidebar. The reason for putting it in your sidebar is that it will appear "sitewide". This means that you would only have to do this once and every post will have your picture on it. It's completely fine if this is something you don't want to do but

I have seen a tremendous increase in conversions since adding one. To add one of your own go to your dashboard and click on "appearance", then click on "widgets".

What you want to do is drag and drop a "text" widget over to your sidebar area and place it somewhere near the top. Under the search box is a great place.

Now go back to your dashboard and click on "posts" in your dashboard's menu. Then click "add new". Once the blank page comes up, don't bother about adding a title or anything. You won't actually be publishing this post. You just need someplace to strip the code from your picture (don't worry, it's easy).

Now you want to click on the "add media" icon.

Once you have done this, you should be given the option to "select media". This will allow you to choose a photo you have stored on your computer (you do have one of those don't you?:).
OK now add the picture to your post (anywhere in the post is fine).

Now that the picture is in the post, click on the "text" tab in the top right corner of the post box like below (some versions of Wordpress will say "html" instead of "text":

Now copy the entire section of code and go back to your widget area and click on the little arrow on the right side of the text widget in your sidebar like in the picture below. Once you have done that, paste the code in the box (where the "x" is). (Yes, that is supposed to be an "x" so stop laughing!:) Once you've done that, click "save" at the bottom of the widget box and then click the little arrow again to close up the text widget.

Now you should be able to visit your site and your snazzy new pic should be in your sidebar!
If the picture box is too big or too small, just go back and adjust the dimensions in the code and save it again.
Now you can go back and delete the post with just your picture on it.
You're done adding a picture to your sidebar!

Quick Tip: When you get to the point that you're ready to add an autoresponder to your blog; placing the email opt-in box will follow the same concept as adding a picture to your sidebar except the code will come from your autoresponder provider (don't worry, their tutorials will walk you through everything).

I want to finish by giving you a template to use when you are making posts. This will give you tremendous leverage with Search Engine Optimization.

SEO Power Post Formula

1. Be sure every post has an H1(header 1) tag containing the keyword phrase you want to rank for. Wordpress does this for you by providing a separate title field for every post.
2. Be sure every post has an H2 & H3 tag containing your keyword phrase.
3. Be sure every post has a picture with your keyword phrase as the alt tag (change up the alt tag if you will use more than 1 pic in the post).
4. Be sure your post is at least 600 words.
5. Be sure your keyword density is 2-5%
6. Try to have an external link using your keyword phrase as the anchor text (the words your visitors will click on). Your website is your homebase and your "business card" to the world. In the next chapter, we are going to talk about setting up an online store but I want to be perfectly clear when I say that you want to definitely maintain your home base website even though you are also creating a store.

The reason I say this is because today's online stores are really good! The functionality is awesome and the prices are reasonable. Most of them also include a blog which would lead you to believe that you don't even need a separate website.

The reason you need to maintain a separate website is that it is YOUR online real estate. Nobody can take it from you and nobody can tell you how to run it. When you blog on the same platform as your online store, you are subject to their terms of service. You are also subject to their lifespan. In other words, if they go out of business or their site crashes for any reason, so does your site and your ENTIRE business with it! This is not something you want to happen, especially when you plan to earn a living from this business.

Now let's go to the next chapter and talk about your online store:)

Chapter 6: Starting an Online Store

Starting an online store was so exciting and fun for me, when I started my online store i present my business on social media and for the first few months it took off like you would never believe. I was going to the post office at least twice a week. Then a few months later I realized I was not getting as much traffic as at the beginning. A part of me felt like I didn't do all I could to keep my customers interested. I also noticed that you need to post a new item at least once a week.

Maintaining an online store is not as easy as you may think. Well at least for me. I really didn't have the time to keep it up like I needed to. When I first started my online store, i was working part time night, so during day I had a lot of time to work my business, do post office runs, order merchandise, book mobile parties at apartment complex and attend special events.It was a lot of work , but it was well worth my time, but most of all it was FUN. I loved shopping for my boutique and plan mobile shows.

One of my first mobile show was at an apartment complex, on a Saturday morning. I had a few customers, but not as much as expected. While there selling, I met a lot of beautiful women who suggest me coming to their church events to sell. The mistake I made with that was I did not reach out to them with information on the events. But, that gave me an idea to host home parties.

My first home party was held at a co-worker's house. That was very challenging. I had no help at all, by the time I got to her house almost all of my furniture in the boutique was moved. I had to set up everything with no help. It was very frustrating, and discouraging. I actually cried trying to set up before everyone got there. My co-worker and her daughter were wonderful assistants and cheerleaders.

After that show I decided that I love doing the shows, it just took a lot out of me driving the boutique and setting up everything with no help. If I could do it all again for the first time I would hire someone to help, definitely have a driver.It's like I couldn't be excited for my customers, I didn't bring energy because of the stress it put me under, trying to get there in one piece and the stress of setting up everything.

A few months later I went on a cousins retreat, I had my best friend to bring my boutique on a day I had designated to set up for a charity event. My best friend was wonderful, he came and helped me , well basically he set everything up for me. I was happy ,full of energy and most of all excited about our event. Everyone enjoyed themselves and it was awesome, at that point i decided that if i could have a successful show like this everytime I did a show it would be awesome. A few weeks later I was offered a manager position on my job. I accepted the position. I knew things would change because my time was limited at this point.

I was thinking one night and it came to me that doing home parties without my boutique would be great. I started networking and asking around and most agreed that having a home party would be of interest to them.

I did my first home show a few weeks later, and when I say that was a great idea, and an awesome show, you better know it.

The most interesting thing was that I had ladies there who loved shopping,and really wore what they bought, as they took pictures while they were at the show and displayed it on their facebook page. Gave me more business!

I thought to myself I think I found the ideal thing to do. I do realize that most people wants to purchase on site. It was like I don't want to shop online I want you to bring it to me, and that's what I did. I took it to the homes of women and had a wonderful night.

Shopify Vs Etsy

A frequent question I get is- Which online store model should I go with? Shopify or Etsy? I think it's a great question to ask and one you certainly want to answer before you spend too much time building an online store and discover it's not the right fit for your product or brand.

When it comes to online stores, both Shopify and Etsy are major players. They are both dwarfed by Amazon but going the Amazon route is something you should consider only after you are sure that your products are selling well online. The reason I say this is because I advocate using the FBA (Fulfilled By Amazon) model if you incorporate Amazon into your online marketing efforts.

Why? Because Amazon has a reputation for lightning fast shipping! Their FBA program requires that you ship the inventory you intend to sell to an actual Amazon warehouse. That way, they have access to your products the moment someone places an order. Amazon takes care of fulfilling the order and you don't have to be chained to your computer or phone waiting on notifications from people purchasing your products on your private store...at 2am!

The thing about using Amazon is that you want to be sure your products have a hungry market before you release your inventory to Amazon. It would be time consuming and frustrating trying to get your unsold inventory back from the Amazon warehouse.

In other words, you want to use Etsy or Shopify to determine the viability of your product and then use Amazon to scale your winning operation.

Now let's look at the major differences between Shopify and Etsy.

Etsy is a complete marketplace for a specific category of products whereas Shopify is a hosted ecommerce platform that you can use to sell literally anything. I would say right up front that the products that tend to do best on Etsy are handmade, one-of-a-kind and bespoke products.

Etsy is a ecommerce store and blog all in one while Shopify is simply a framework that allows you the ability to set up a storefront on your website. In plain words, Etsy would be a completely furnished building with land, a parking lot, electricity and running water. Shopify, on the other hand would one of those steel buildings that you can buy and put on your land, furnish it and supply your own power and running water.

They both have their merits and whether one is better than the other would depend on your use for them. If you already have an established website but just want to add an ecommerce store, Shopify may be your next best step.

Whereas you can see 1000 shopify stores and not see the same one twice, it doesn't take but a few different Etsy store visits to let you know that there are some limitations on making your Etsy store unique. This isn't necessarily a bad thing as Etsy is a respected and established brand with a fabulous look and feel to it's storefront. Instead of feeling like you're not standing out from the pack, you should really feel a sense of confidence because of the familiarity and reassurance your customers will feel knowing they are shopping on a trusted Etsy site. Custom URLs

As far as URLs are concerned, Shopify will give you a shopify url for free but it's really meant to be temporary until you buy and link your own custom url to your Shopify store. Etsy on the other hand, doesn't give you many options for customized urls except when you use their premium service which allows you to link your Etsy store to your website.

Fees & Pricing

It has been said that you get what you pay for. That applies to ecommerce too. While there are lots of free tools and solutions online, I don't advise using free platforms when it comes to running your business.

Whenever you use a tool or piece of software created and managed by someone else, you are subject to it changing ot going away completely. That applies ten fold to free tools and software. Take my word for it, you definitely want to pay for your ecommerce solution.

Etsy and Shopify take drastically different approaches to their pricing models.

With Shopify, you pay a flat fee per month starting at $29/mo. This fee includes hosting and support. You do not pay transaction fees to Shopify outside of credit card processing fees. The great thing about that is that is doesn't matter how many products you display in your store or how much bandwidth your store takes up. In other words, your store can do millions of dollars a year in revenue and you will still pay $29/Mo.

With Etsy, an account & storefront are free. You pay $0.20 to list items for sale and pay a 3.5% transaction fee per sale *plus* credit card fees. Adding a Patterns site w/ a custom domain adds a $15/mo fee. With this pricing model, you would pay .20 for each product you list. So for every 100 items you list in your store, you would pay a total of $20 and then 3.5% of the sales price when each item is sold. Of course you could build the 3.5% fee into your cost per item and pass this fee on to your customers. The choice is yours.
Getting Traffic

With any online business, your ability to get customer's eyeballs looking at your offering is key. The online equivalent of customers coming into your brick-and-and mortar store is traffic or unique visits to your website or online store.

I strongly advise you to take personal responsibility for your traffic. It's not up to google to send you traffic. Google's job is to connect those searching for a particular service or product with the very best services and products available. It's your job to create the best products and services and to make sure they are seen by your target audience.

With respect to Etsy and Shopify, let's consider the following:

With Shopify, you are responsible for driving visitors to your site. You have to develop an effective marketing plan and execute on it. Shopify provides a very SEO-friendly platform to work with but this alone will not put your site in front of the masses.
With Etsy, the story is a little different. They advertise and bring in customers to the marketplace in addition to any visitors that you bring directly to your Etsy shop. In fact, *many customers start their search on Etsy* for an Etsy shop. They are pre-sold on buying from an Etsy shop – you simply have to have what they want.

Think of Etsy as a shop in the mall and Shopify as an obscure boutique hidden in the boonies. Just because Etsy has the advantage over Shopify, that doesn't give you permission to think your Etsy shop is a set-and-forget affair. Your should still have a paid traffic campaign planned for whatever platform you choose. You just have a boost when it comes to Etsy.

Rules & Limitations

With Shopify, you can sell basically whatever you want, subject to your local laws and Shopify's terms of service (ie, no illegal substances, content or objects). You can sell your own stuff and also list complementary manufactured products. It's your store that you can run based on your business goals.

With Etsy, you are subject to their marketplace rules, which limit products to handmade, vintage and artisanal goods. If you want to cross sell or upsell complementary manufactured products – then Etsy isn't for you.

And like the design limitations, you are limited to how you list and present your products. Etsy has a specific process for listing products. There's no changing or opting out. You have tons more options with Shopify where design is concerned.

Inventory & Payment Processing

With Shopify, you have a full inventory management system that syncs with your customers and orders. Shopify also has their own payment processing service and point-of-sale service, so you can sync your offline sales with your inventory on Shopify.
Etsy, again, is a marketplace, not a platform. You list products for sale (and pay per listing) but you have to maintain inventory records elsewhere. There are 3rd party apps that can link to Etsy but the management will be with the 3rd party app – not integrated into Etsy.

Regardless which route you take in choosing your payment processing method, be sure to keep an eye towards a seamless transition for your customers. That includes your shipping method.

Mobile Boutique Home Parties

I've saved the best for last. I have, by far, experienced the most success by using my mobile boutique to perform home parties. It's a great way to showcase your products to a hungry market and it's also a great way to get instant feedback on the products you currently carry as well as what your audience would life for you to carry in the future.

Even though you stand to make more money over the long term by selling online, home parties are a great way to begin. It's more work and you have to interact with more people personally but it gives a great feeling of satisfaction to see women happy with their purchases. Keep in mind, you're not just selling them jewelry, you're selling them a more beautiful appearance!

One downside to home parties is that you can only do one at a time. Another one is that they require your physical presence. It doesn't take too many of these before your awesome business starts to feel like a job.

This is why you need to be passionate about what you're doing. I recommend keeping your home party schedule in tune with the work/life balance you desire.
Many hosts will want to book parties on the weekend. He last thing you want to do is to look up and realize you haven't had a weekend with your family in 3 months! Be careful! The money isn't worth it at the end of the day. I know it seems like I'm bashing the mobile boutique business. I'm not. I'm only warning those who would let the profits get in the way of what matters most.

Advertising
You not only advertise for the show, you also advertise at the show(product displays and lighting).

Advertising for your home party show may be easier than you think. Instead of convincing 25 ladies that your home party is the place to be, you really only have to convince one- the Hostess! That's right! If you do your part, the owner of the home will do all the advertising for you. You may have to provide business cards and some sales literature but they will be your chief marketer for that particular show.

Your goal is to find as many hostesses to book your home parties with as possible.
Client Wish List

The Hostess knows best! Trying to figure out what products to offer in your home party will require you to tap into the mind of the hostess. She knows the style of the people she's inviting to the party. She already has a sense of what her friends and coworkers like and would be a better judge of what you should put on display than you are.

It would be good to sit down with her well in advance and discuss what will be displayed during the party. Be careful here though, you don't want them getting all whimsical on you. This could lead to you ordering jewelry pieces that are completely outside of what you are used to buying. You could wind up with pieces so unique that no one would buy them. Then you would be stuck with it long after the party is over. Not cool! Try to blend your style with the Hostess' style and don't let them get too far outside the box when choosing jewelry pieces.

A good client wish list will mean more sales and more profits.
Profit Split

One of the greatest things about home parties is that everyone wins. The Hostess wins because she provided a great experience for her friends and neighbors. The guests win because they get treated like royalty. And you win because you not only earn a very decent profit for the evening, you also potentially gain prospects...for future profits!

Every now and then though, you will encounter a nervous or unenthusiastic Hostess. I have found that nothing gets the Hostess on your side like a profit share. There's no need to go off the deep end here with a 50/50 split. I would probably not even bring up a profit split if there are less than 20 guests. If the Hostess has gone out of her way to rent a facility and there are over 20 guests, I would normally offer 10%-15% plus her choice of one of the jewelry pieces. This would normally apply to organized groups like women's ministries or sororities.

Home Preview
Once you've booked a home party, you will definitely need

to go by the home and get the lay of the land. Will it be best to work out of your mobile boutique? Will the room support large or small displays? What size tables will work with the space you're planning for?

All these questions need to definitely be answered beforehand. It's critically important for you to personally view the home or facility. This will eliminate you trying to imagine your equipment in a space that was described to you verbally. Few things say "unprofessional" than a makeshift setup.

Plan in advance and be the boss you know you are!
Set-Up

When you do get to the setup phase of your home party, you want to be very strategic when it comes to displaying your jewelry. I have found that mixing the expensive pieces with the inexpensive pieces works best. In fact, the expensive pieces help the inexpensive pieces look more expensive. You will probably find that if you separate the inexpensive pieces from the expensive pieces, you will sell one category but not the other.

You also want the purchase process to be as easy as possible. I use Square and have never had an issue. Whatever you choose, make sure it is compatible with Apple and Android products. You also want to be able to make change for those paying with cash. Also have receipts on hand and offer them for every purchase.

Only offer a return policy for defective pieces. You don't want to offer a blanket return policy. People buy these types of pieces on impulse and a blanket return policy is not necessary.

You can mix and match your home parties with your other income methods. I have found that home parties are a great way to validate products and get clients through word of mouth.

Conclusion

Whether you want to earn an extra few hundred dollars per week or you want to replace your income entirely, a mobile boutique business can be just the ticket. The mobile boutique business is one that rewards planning ahead and great customer service skills. It is a thriving industry with a hungry market.

I hope that this book has in some way inspired, encouraged and informed you for your upcoming mobile boutique adventures.

I wish you all the best!